AF441785

Songs in the Night

Songs in the Night

A 31-Day Journey through
Music and Healing

SUSAN M. FERGUSON

Aneko Press

www.anekopress.com

inquiries@anekopress.com

Aneko Press, Life Sentence Publishing, and our logos are trademarks of

Life Sentence Publishing, Inc.
203 E. Birch Street
P.O. Box 652
Abbotsford, WI 54405

RELIGION / Christian Living / Inspirational

Paperback ISBN: 979-8-88936-542-6

eBook ISBN: 979-8-88936-543-3

10 9 8 7 6 5 4 3 2 1

Available where books are sold

Contents

But each day the Lord pours his unfailing love upon me, and through each night I sing his songs, praying to God who gives me life.

When Music Became My Medicine

I never expected to spend thirty-one days in a hospital room, surrounded by the steady hum of machines, the sharp scent of antiseptic, and the constant rhythm of nurses' footsteps in the hall. Each day brought its own battle – pain, uncertainty, loneliness, and fear. But through it all, one thing remained constant: Christ and His never-ending, never-deserting presence.

In my hospital room, it was the power of worship music that carried me. Music that kept my mind, my thoughts, and my heart focused on the truth of God. It filled my room and wrapped around my heart like a warm blanket. It lifted my eyes when I could barely open them, whispered hope when fear was loud, and reminded me that even here – especially here – God was with me.

Music became more than background noise. It became a lifeline, a form of prayer, a way to say what my tired body and anxious heart could not. Some days, a single lyric was enough to keep me grounded. Other days, an entire worship set helped me fall asleep in peace instead of panic.

This book is the story of those thirty-one days – not just the medical journey but the spiritual path I walked (or sometimes simply survived) with the help of God-inspired music. Each chapter represents a day, a song, a struggle, and a breakthrough. It is a testimony to the power of worship in the hardest places.

If you are reading this in your own hospital room or in a season of pain, I pray that what brought me comfort might bring you comfort as well. May these songs become your songs. May this story remind you that you are never alone. And may you hear, even in the silence, the voice of God singing over you.

Battle Belongs

"When all I see is the battle,
You see my victory . . ."

– Phil Wickham, "Battle Belongs"

The timing was no accident.
I closed my eyes and listened:

"So when I fight, I'll fight on my knees
With my hands lifted high . . ."

As I went to the orthopedic hospital for knee replacement surgery, I had a clear plan for healing and recovery. I expected to be home the next day, begin therapy the following week, and within six weeks, move around with little discomfort.

We arrived at the surgical center early in the morning and soon met with the orthopedist and the anesthesia team. The surgery went well, and I woke up a few hours later. The nurses had me up and walking that same afternoon. All good.

What I did not realize was that a battle lay ahead.

As this song played in my room, it reminded me of something I needed to hear: God knows every battle we face, and we do not fight alone. In that hospital room I was not abandoned. God was with me. He saw what lay ahead – victory.

Day 1 was the beginning of a long journey, but it was also the start of a deeper faith. And it began with a song that declared the truth I needed most:

The battle belongs to God.

Psalm 34:19

The righteous person faces many troubles,
but the Lord comes to the rescue each time.

'Tis So Sweet

"'Tis so sweet to trust in Jesus,
Just to take Him at His word . . ."

– Shane & Shane, "'Tis So Sweet"

I woke up on the second day with pain in my ribs and chest. The nurses helped me walk in the halls as part of my therapy, and I even took some breathing treatments, but something just wasn't right.

After the doctor examined me that afternoon, he said I needed to stay another day so I could be monitored. The rib pain was increasing, and chest X-rays and other tests followed.

The adrenaline of day one had worn off, and reality started to settle in: this wasn't going to be over soon. There were too many unknowns. How long would I be here? Would my body heal fully?

And in that waiting, fear tried to take over.

But then the music began to play again.

This time, the hymn "'Tis So Sweet" floated through the air – slow, tender, and familiar. Every word met me in my need:

> "Just to rest upon His promise,
> Just to know, 'Thus saith the Lord.'"

I needed to rest – not just physically but spiritually. I needed to trust that Jesus was holding me, even when I felt like I was falling apart.

There is something powerful about simple trust. Not because everything makes sense but because Jesus is trustworthy, even when the circumstances are not. That hymn reminded me that faith doesn't need all the answers – it just needs the right anchor.

And my anchor was Christ.

That day, I made a decision: I would listen. I would feed my soul. If I couldn't move, I would let the music move in me.

I didn't have the energy or desire to journal, use my computer, or read, but I could listen. So with my phone next to my ear, I listened to my playlists and was gently comforted.

That day I closed my eyes and let the words of the hymn settle over me like a lullaby:

> "Jesus, Jesus, how I trust Him,
> How I've proved Him o'er and o'er . . ."

Day 2 wasn't easy, but it did grow sweeter. Because I chose to lean into Jesus – not the fear, not the questions, not the pain. Just Jesus.

My mind wanted answers, but all I had was waiting. And that was enough.

Philippians 4:6

Don't worry about anything; instead, pray about everything. Tell God what you need, and thank him for all he has done.

He Will Hold Me Fast

"When I fear my faith will fail,
Christ will hold me fast . . ."

– Shane & Shane, "He Will Hold Me Fast"

Day 3 revealed a new challenge: A CT scan showed that my trachea and esophagus had been perforated during the anesthesia intubation, causing serious complications in my chest cavity. Unfortunately, the hospital where I had my surgery was not equipped to treat this type of injury.

All eating and drinking by mouth was abruptly stopped.

By late afternoon, the process of transferring me to another hospital had begun. The staff searched for a facility with the capability to diagnose and treat the damage. In those hours of waiting, the need not to fear became even greater.

Finally, late in the evening, the ground transfer began, though it took hours to complete. As I lay on the transport bed, listening to the wheels turn beneath me and the soft beeping of machines, my mind spun with anxiety. I didn't know what to expect next.

At the new hospital, more tests followed – and they were not pleasant. My knee replacement, the very reason for the surgery, quickly faded into the background as everything shifted to the complications in my chest.

Then I heard the song: "He Will Hold Me Fast."

Whether it was playing on a playlist or simply echoing in my heart, I'm not sure. But I heard it.

> "When the tempter would prevail,
> He will hold me fast."

And I knew it was true.

I didn't have to hold everything together. I didn't have to be strong. I didn't even have to understand what would happen next. Because He was holding me – not just in theory but in the most literal sense. Christ was carrying me from one hospital to another, from one moment of weakness to the next breath of grace.

I could not eat or drink, and my mouth was painfully dry. My throat hurt. My heart felt heavy.

In a world that suddenly felt unstable, God became my stability. That song wrapped itself around my trembling soul and reminded me that I was not falling apart – I was being held.

"For my Savior loves me so,
He will hold me fast."

Day 3 reminded me that change is hard. But trust is holy.
Even when everything around me shifted, He did not.

Psalm 139:9–10 (NIV)

*If I rise on the wings of the dawn, if I settle on
the far side of the sea, even there your hand
will guide me, your right hand will hold me fast.*

I Will Wait for You (Psalm 130)

"I will wait for You, I will wait for You,
On Your word I will rely."

– Shane & Shane, "I Will Wait
for You (Psalm 130)"

Day 4 took everything to another level. It felt as if every step forward came with two steps back. The physical pain was increasing, but the emotional fatigue was even worse.

Each procedure brought a new kind of discomfort – tubes adjusted, needles pressed into veins, more scans, and a very uncomfortable awake bronchoscopy. Every movement seemed to waken another nerve.

Eventually I was taken into an operating room. My new cardiothoracic surgeon and anesthesiologist used a camera to examine my damaged esophagus and tracheal airways before beginning the planned surgery to repair a hole that was allowing air to leak into my chest cavity. But the examination revealed internal perforations and swelling. Because of the damage, the breathing tube required for surgery could not be safely inserted.

It was also the weekend, so the decision was made to move me again – this time to one of the trauma hospitals in North Texas that could handle my now very serious condition. I needed more advanced care, and a completely new treatment plan would have to be developed with additional specialists.

I remember lying there, trying to process the news. That word – *trauma* – hit me hard. It made everything feel more real. Another hospital. Another medical team. More questions, more procedures, more unknowns. I didn't know how or why this had happened, and I didn't have answers.

I didn't feel strong. I didn't feel brave. My body felt broken, as if it no longer belonged to me, and the exhaustion of it all weighed heavily on my spirit.

But as I waited in the ICU before the transport arrived, prayers for my situation were spreading quickly. Friends, churches in several states, and even people in other countries were praying.

My friend Russ asked me a simple question: "Are you afraid?"

I answered honestly, "No."

I knew God would either heal me or take me to heaven. Either outcome was good. And somehow, in that moment, God gave me peace.

That day the song "I Will Wait for You" by Shane & Shane became my quiet prayer.

The transport came in the middle of the night. The ride was rough. I was strapped down, still unable to eat or drink. I was weak, weary, and my injuries caused intense pain in my chest.

And so, I waited.

In that moment, when all sense of control had been stripped away, I heard the soft, familiar words of the song:

"I will wait for You, I will wait for You,
On Your word I will rely.
I will wait for You, surely wait for You
Till my soul is satisfied."

I didn't have to be brave or composed. I didn't have to have answers. I could come to Jesus exactly as I was – frightened, hurting, and worn out.

He wasn't waiting for me to get stronger first.

He was already there, riding in the back of that ambulance with me.

That ride to the trauma hospital marked one of my lowest moments physically. But spiritually, it became one of the most intimate. There was no pretending. No performance. Just surrender.

And that was enough.

Because when I had nothing left to give, I learned something important: God never asked me to bring strength – only trust.

That day I learned that worship is not always loud. Sometimes it is the quiet surrender of a wounded soul whispering, "I still trust You. I will wait for You."

Day 4 was filled with pain but also with a strange kind of peace – the kind that comes when you know you are loved exactly as you are.

Psalm 130:1

From the depths of despair,
O LORD, I call for your help.

Day 5

Psalm 46 (Lord of Hosts)

"You will lead us,
Through the fiercest battle."

– Shane & Shane, "Psalm 46
(Lord of Hosts)"

I arrived at the trauma hospital just after midnight on Day 5. Amazing nurses met me at the door and said, "We've been waiting for you!" Their caring faces eased my fears and made me feel both comfortable and seen. I was taken to the ICU, and the seriousness of my condition began to settle in.

The trauma team confirmed what the previous doctors suspected: My esophagus and trachea were damaged, and I would require surgery once the swelling had been reduced with IV medications and additional testing was completed. The words *thoracic surgery* echoed in my mind like a thunderclap. I wasn't sure how I would heal or how long this ordeal would last.

Everything felt fragile – my body, my voice, even my hope.

But then something happened that steadied me again.

My husband, my two sons, and my daughter-in-love walked into the room. Their presence brought joy and renewed hope to my soul.

I didn't have much energy to speak, but I didn't need to. Their presence itself was a kind of healing. They held my hand, prayed over me, and reminded me through their eyes and gentle touch that I was not facing this alone. Love has a language of its own, and that day it spoke clearly.

In the background, I had "Psalm 46" by Shane & Shane playing softly. When the chorus began, it felt as if heaven had opened:

> "Lord of hosts, You're with us,
> With us in the fire,
> With us as a shelter,
> With us in the storm."

Tears welled in my eyes – not out of fear but out of thankfulness. Even in the ICU, with surgery ahead and tubes still tangled around my body, I felt a calmness rising in my chest.

I was not alone in the fire.

God was my refuge – not just conceptually but tangibly. He was present in that hospital room. He was in the hands of the doctors and nurses, in the quiet strength of my family, and in the peace filling my spirit as the music played.

> "Oh, where else would we go,
> But with the Lord of Hosts?"

Day 5 stood on the edge of something serious. I didn't know what surgery would bring.
But I knew this: God was already in tomorrow.
And tonight, He was right there with me.

Psalm 46:1

God is our refuge and strength,
always ready to help in times of trouble.

Hope Has a Name

"Hope has a name. His name is Jesus.
My Savior's cross has set this sinner free . . ."

– River Valley Worship, "Hope Has a Name"

And then, as if on cue, the words of the song echoed in my mind:

"Hope has a name. His name is Jesus.
Oh, Christ be praised; I have victory."

In that moment, I didn't feel victorious in the way the world defines victory. I was hurting.

"There is a song. I know it well.
A melody that's never failed . . ."

That morning, Jesus became my melody.

And, even in the pain, I was victorious.

Not because everything was fixed and not because the fear had disappeared but because hope was holding me through the darkness. I knew I was in Jesus's hands – my Hope.

In my mind, I pictured Him there beside me, dressed like a surgeon in scrubs, tears in His eyes, holding my hand and calling me beloved.

Day 6 would be the day I prepared for surgery. But more than that, it would be the day I woke up again to the power of hope.

Hope is not wishful thinking.

Hope has a name.

And His name is Jesus.

Psalm 46:7

The Lord *of Heaven's Armies is here among us; the God of Israel is our fortress.*

Day 7

In Christ Alone

"In Christ alone my hope is found,
He is my light, my strength, my song . . ."

– Shane & Shane, In Christ Alone

The seventh day.

I was wheeled into surgery and later learned that my dear family and friends had gathered to pray and wait during the procedure. I am deeply thankful for loved ones who call out to God on my behalf.

In Christ alone my hope is found. I trusted the team involved in my surgery, but I also knew Christ Himself was in that operating room.

When I woke up, my body was in pain and my mind was foggy, but I was alive. I could feel four tubes protruding from my back, pulling and pressing against my skin with every breath. I was groggy and disoriented . . . and yet, in a strange way, at peace.

Because when I opened my eyes, my husband and sons were standing beside me.

They didn't have to say a word. Their presence said everything: *You made it. We're here. You're not alone.*

The tubes tugged painfully whenever I tried to shift. My body felt sore, heavy, and stitched together – physically and emotionally. I had to rely on nurses for nearly everything. Even the smallest task, like sitting up, felt like climbing a mountain.

And yet, I was still here.

Still breathing.

Still believing.

Still healing.

By this point I knew the recovery would not be quick, as we so often hope. The road ahead was long, and I was only at the beginning. But I had come through the valley of surgery, and I was waking up with a deeper realization: My hope was not in doctors, procedures, or test results.

Even though my cardiothoracic surgeon, knee surgeon, ENT surgeon, and the nursing staff were wonderful, my hope was in Christ alone.

Later I was told that the abscess just above my heart and right lung had been serious. The surgeon said I should have been much sicker going into that thoracic surgery. But we knew Christ had protected me.

That song, "In Christ Alone," played quietly through my speaker as the morning light filtered into my ICU room. The words were no longer just lyrics; they were my reality.

"This cornerstone, this solid ground,
Firm through the fiercest
drought and storm . . ."

Jesus was my cornerstone – unshaken, unmovable – even when everything in my world had been turned upside down. The storm had not stopped, but I had found shelter in Him.

"No power of hell, no scheme of man,
Can ever pluck me from His hand . . ."

That line struck me deeply.

I felt weak, vulnerable, and small. But in that moment I knew this with all my heart: I was safe in His hands.

Not because of my strength,
but because of His.

Day 7 reminded me of something that would become a theme in the days ahead: Christ is enough. Not only when life is good but especially when it isn't. He was with me in every monitor beep, every shift change, and every breath that hurt to take.

In Christ alone my hope is found.

Psalm 33:22

*Let your unfailing love surround us,
Lord, for our hope is in you alone.*

Psalm 23 (Surely Goodness, Surely Mercy)

"The Lord is my shepherd;
I shall not want . . ."

– Shane & Shane, "Psalm 23
(Surely Goodness, Surely Mercy)"

Today I rested in the words of Psalm 23. The familiar promises brought peace: green pastures, still waters, and the restoration of the soul.

The LORD is my shepherd; I have all that I need. He lets me rest in green meadows; He leads me beside peaceful streams. He renews my strength. He guides me along right paths, bringing honor to his name. Even when I walk through the darkest valley, I will not be afraid, for you are close beside me (Psalm 23:1-4).

Eight days in, and each one had felt like a mountain.

I had a PICC line inserted in my left arm today. It was an uncomfortable procedure, but it would now provide easier access for the medications I needed.

But Day 8 brought something I hadn't expected: a sense of calm. Not because the pain was gone or the road ahead was suddenly clear. In fact, the day brought new challenges and more questions – but also more reminders that I wasn't alone.

My family had been there since the beginning, and they faithfully remained with me. One of them was always by my side. They rotated shifts like quiet warriors, never letting me face a moment alone. They prayed with me, held my hand, and sat in silence when words weren't needed. Just their presence helped me breathe a little easier.

And then there were the nurses.

I couldn't say enough about them. These incredible men and women didn't just care for my body; they cared for me. With gentleness and grace, they handled every tube, every bandage, every painful moment as if it were sacred. In the darkest nights, they were the hands and heart of Jesus, moving with compassion and confidence.

"Surely goodness, surely mercy,
Right beside me all my days,
And I will dwell in Your house forever,
And bless Your holy name."

The truth of Psalm 23 wrapped around my soul like a warm blanket.

I didn't need to strive. I didn't need to fear.

Day 8. The Lord is my Shepherd. That is enough.

Psalm 23:4

Even when I walk through the darkest valley,
I will not be afraid, for you are close beside me.

Day 9

Give Me Jesus

"In the morning when I rise,
Give me Jesus."

– Shane & Shane, "Give Me Jesus"

"Give Me Jesus" by Shane & Shane played softly as I was wheeled out for a test – a swallow study to see whether my damaged esophagus was healing.

It was simple but emotionally and physically challenging. I had to stand for the test, and I was weak after surgery. By this point I had gone seven days without food or drink by mouth. Even water had been forbidden. But the hope was that maybe – just maybe – I would be able to take a small step forward.

The results came back: not yet. The hole in my esophagus had not closed. I still couldn't swallow safely.

But . . . I was allowed ice chips.

If I didn't swallow them, I could let them cool my mouth before spitting them out. And I cried.

I know that sounds small. But after days without anything passing my lips, those tiny, cold chips felt like a gift from heaven – a miracle in miniature. I sat in my hospital bed, letting them melt slowly and savoring the moment.

> "You can have all this world,
> But give me Jesus."

Because no matter how many people surrounded me, how many machines were keeping me going, or how many ice cubes soothed my dry mouth, only Jesus could give me the strength I truly needed. Only He could calm my racing thoughts and give purpose to my pain.

I didn't need answers.

I didn't need control.

I just needed Him.

That afternoon I took another important step forward: I was moved from the ICU to the Progressive Care Unit (PCU).

It may not sound like much, but it was huge. ICU had become familiar. I knew the rhythm, the faces, the nighttime routines. Moving meant progress – but it also meant change. After so many days of being watched around the clock, part of me felt nervous leaving that constant care behind.

But I quickly discovered that the PCU nurses and aides were just as compassionate, attentive, and gentle as the team in ICU. They made me feel safe and seen.

Later that day I was reminded that another swallow test was coming in a few days. I wasn't there yet. The finish line wasn't in sight. But I was moving forward.

And I was not alone.

"When I come to die,
Give me Jesus."

That line hit deeply.

Because even in moments that felt like death – the death of control, the death of comfort, the death of the life I once knew – Jesus was the only thing that truly sustained me. He wasn't just with me.

He was enough for me.

Day 9 was hard.

But it was holy.

Psalm 59:16

But as for me, I will sing about your power.
Each morning, I will sing with joy about your
unfailing love. For you have been my refuge,
a place of safety when I am in distress.

Day 10

Psalm 139 (Far Too Wonderful)

"You see me through and
through and call me loved,
What a wonderful grace . . ."

– Shane & Shane, "Psalm 139
(Far Too Wonderful)"

"Oh, I can't run, I can't hide,
Even darkness is a light,
From the lowest place,
To the highest praise,
You are worthy."

The morning of Day 10 began like most of the others: dim lights, nurses checking vitals, and monitors beeping steadily in the background.

But today there was a new challenge waiting for me – therapy.

My husband, Sam, and my sons, Michael and Andrew, had kept the ice machine running on my knee while I rested in bed. Now it was time to start moving.

My body was still sore from surgery. The tubes in my back tugged with every movement. I was connected to drains, monitors, IVs, and oxygen. And now I was being asked to get out of bed and walk.

It felt impossible.

But I wanted to try.

With the help of therapists and nurses – and the encouragement of my family – I slowly swung my legs over the edge of the bed. It wasn't just my knee and chest that needed healing; my whole body had been through trauma.

Still, inch by inch, I stood.

With every shaky step down the hallway, a parade of people and equipment followed me – poles, tubes, wires, machines. It wasn't graceful, and it definitely wasn't fast. But it was forward. My family even documented each session with photos.

As the day went on, another bright moment arrived: My daughter-in-love Virginia and three of my grandchildren came to visit.

Their presence was a gift – a glimpse of normal life, joy, and innocence inside hospital walls. They saw the wires and the beeping machines, but they also saw me.

And my granddaughter Hadleigh did something I will never forget.

She washed my hair.

There I was – weak, bandaged, and dependent on others for even the most basic things – and my sweet granddaughter stepped in to serve me with such gentleness and love. With a warm shampoo cap and careful hands, she restored a sense of dignity I hadn't even realized I was missing.

The simple act of having clean, brushed hair made me feel human again.

Cared for.

Known.

"Psalm 139" played quietly in the background, and as I listened I remembered: He saw every part of me – every wound, every weary sigh, every struggle to walk, every tear that fell in silence.

> "Amazing love, how can it be?
> Far too wonderful for me.
> There's only one thing left to say:
> You are worthy."

Even there, in a hospital bed – tethered to machines, progress measured in slow steps and ice chips – He was with me. Not just watching. Not just present. But actively hemming me in, surrounding me with His love, holding me fast.

That is what Day 10 became: a day of being known.

Not just by family.

But by God.

Psalm 139:1

*O LORD, you have examined my heart
and know everything about me.*

Day 11

No One Ever Cared for Me Like Jesus

"If my heart could tell a story,
If my life would sing a song,
If I have a testimony,
If I have anything at all."

– Steffany Gretzinger, "No One
Ever Cared for Me Like Jesus"

The nights were the hardest.

By Day 11, I had come to expect that sleep would arrive only in pieces – if at all. There were constant interruptions: nurses checking vitals, blood draws, injections, machines beeping, and the steady thud of footsteps in the hallway. Around 5:30 a.m., like clockwork, came the chest X-ray . . . a ritual I had begun to anticipate with weary acceptance.

Everything hurt more at night. The silence felt louder. The room seemed colder. The loneliness crept in deeper.

Softly, near my ear, my music played – steady, comforting, close. And every night, without fail, I listened as the songs soothed me. That night, one in particular whispered to my soul:

"No one ever cared for me like Jesus . . ."

My husband and sons faithfully remained with me – caring for me, fighting for me, and praying for me.

And then she walked in.

My daughter, Erica, finally well after recovering from the flu, came to be with me. She had stayed away to protect me, to give me the best chance at healing without complications. Seeing her in person after so many days apart felt like sunlight breaking through thick clouds.

I cried.

I smiled.

I held her hand.

And I relaxed, knowing she was there.

"Let my children tell their children;
Let this be their memory:
That all my treasure was in heaven,
And You were everything to me."

This battle I was in wasn't mine to win alone. I wasn't strong enough on my own – and thankfully, I didn't have to be.

I fought by resting.

I fought by trusting.

I fought by worshiping in the silence, even when the outcome was still unclear.

I fought by receiving love – from nurses, from my husband and family, and that day, from my daughter.

There's something about suffering that strips everything else away. What once seemed important fades into the background. And what remains – the true anchor – is Jesus.

The One who holds you when the IV alarms won't stop.

The One who sees the bruises from blood draws and endless injections into my abdomen and still calls you beloved.

The One who stays up through the night with you, whispering, "You're not alone."

By the time the sun began to rise – my favorite moment of each day – I felt a new strength. Not physical. But deep. Quiet. Sure.

On Day 11, I was surrounded by love – the care of family and nurses. But I also knew something even deeper.

No one had ever cared for me like Jesus.

Psalm 145:4

*Let each generation tell its children of your
mighty acts; let them proclaim your power.*

Day 12

Only There

"Only there, only there,
Love and mercy flow for me."

– Shane & Shane, "Only There"

*D*ay 12 began with a quiet sense of expectation. The weight of another swallow test loomed ahead. It would take place tomorrow, but the emotional toll had already begun.

These tests weren't just medical milestones. They felt like measuring sticks for my healing, and each one brought its own storm of hope, fear, and fragile resolve.

As "Only There" played gently in the background, I felt the profound truth of the lyrics wash over me: Love and mercy truly do flow from the cross – not just in eternity, but here, in this room, on this hard day.

I rested.

I trusted.

And as I looked toward the next day's test, I whispered a quiet but powerful prayer:

"Lord, I trust You. I don't know what the results will be, but I know You're already there."

I rested with worship.

With surrender.

With ice chips in my mouth and Scripture in my soul.

And most of all, I rested in the presence of Jesus, who never left my side.

I remembered where my true healing flowed from: only there.

> "I find my rest (only there).
> I find my peace (only there).
> I find my hope (only there).
> I'm finding everything I need."

That chorus echoed softly through my phone speaker.

> "Only there, only there,
> Love and mercy flow for me.
> Only there, only there
> Can I find my rest in Thee."

I rested in every prayer lifted on my behalf.

With every kind word from a nurse.

With every visit from family.

With every worship song played softly through the night.

Day 12 reminded me that victory doesn't always look like instant healing. Sometimes it looks like progress.

A visit from someone you love. A breath that comes a little easier. A nurse who calls you by name. A God who surrounds you on every side.

Matthew 11:28

Then Jesus said, "Come to me, all of you who are weary and carry heavy burdens, and I will give you rest."

Where I'm Standing Now

"Out of the wilderness,
Into Your deliverance,
Look where I'm standing now."

– Phil Wickham, "Where I'm Standing Now"

Day 13 was quiet but full of reflection. The swallow test came, and I knew from the radiologist's response that once again I hadn't passed.

My heart sank.

So much waiting. So much hope wrapped around one test. I had longed for the moment when I could finally eat or drink again – even the smallest sip. But the preliminary results made it clear: My esophagus still wasn't healed.

I still couldn't eat or drink, but ice chips remained a small joy.

It's amazing how something so simple can bring

such comfort. I would hold each chip in my mouth, letting it melt slowly – refreshing and familiar – before spitting it out.

A small mercy.

And I was comforted.

> "I stand on the chain-breaking,
> Miracle-making,
> Powerful name of Jesus,
> On the body-raising,
> Prodigal-saving,
> Powerful name of Jesus."

I felt tired. My body was still tethered to tubes. The simple act of walking still required effort, and progress was measured in small, sometimes invisible steps.

But I realized something important: Flourishing isn't always loud.

Sometimes it looks like faithfulness in affliction.

Sometimes it looks like holding on to praise in a hospital bed.

Sometimes it sounds like soft worship music playing through the night.

And sometimes it looks like still believing God is good – even when healing is slow.

My family came again – my husband, son, and daughter faithfully at my side. They listened carefully to every doctor and cared for my needs in every way. Their presence made the sterile hospital room feel a little more like home, and I treasured every moment with them.

There's nothing quite like a family's presence, no matter how grown they are.

They sat with me, talked with me, looked into my eyes, and reminded me of who I was outside those hospital walls. Even though I was still surrounded by monitors, tubes, and procedures, I was also surrounded by love.

Dr. Kristi faithfully came each day to check on me and give updates. Her presence brought a calm assurance, and she never seemed to be in a hurry. When she came in that day, she told me she had been praying for me and asked if she could pray with me right then.

Oh, what a precious gift – to be prayed for!

All praise to God for that moment – for that hospital, for Kristi, and for that prayer.

Praise became my purpose.

Worship became my weapon.

And God's presence became my peace.

Because even in the nights when I was poked and prodded . . .

Even in the tests that brought discouraging news . . .

Even in the weariness of therapy and waiting . . .

God had not left me.

And that alone was reason to give thanks.

As "Where I'm Standing Now" played on Day 13, I realized how far God had already brought me. I wasn't fully healed yet, but I wasn't where I started either.

There was wreckage – but He was rebuilding.

There was weakness – but I was still standing.

And where I was standing . . .

was on grace.

2 Timothy 4:17

*But the Lord stood with me
and gave me strength.*

Praise the Name of Jesus

"Praise the name of Jesus,
Praise the name of Jesus.
He's my rock, He's my fortress,
He's my deliverer;
In Him shall I trust . . ."

– Shane & Shane, "Praise
the Name of Jesus"

Day 14 began like any other morning in the PCU. The chest X-ray came at 5:30, followed by nurses drawing blood, giving injections and medications, and then the usual doctor visits. The routine had become wearying yet predictable.

My husband, Sam, and son Andrew had the flu, so I wouldn't be seeing them for a few days.

And then . . . God stepped in.

Not with flashing lights or dramatic miracles, but

with three close friends, warm smiles, arms full of gifts, and hearts full of prayer.

They entered my hospital room like a wave of fresh air. Laughter bubbled up for the first time in days. There were hugs, stories, tears, and a sacred kind of comfort that only friendship can bring. They didn't need to say anything profound. Their presence was the miracle.

My friend Sharon brought smiles, prayers, flowers, and lotion. Then Sue and Marty brought hope of normal life and a gift from my Bible study group. It was a basket full of practical, thoughtful things that reminded me I was still myself, even in a hospital gown.

But the gift that touched my heart the most was a wooden sign tucked inside the basket. It simply read:

"And then God stepped in."

I held it in my hands, tears welling up in my eyes, and whispered in my heart,

"Yes, He did."

He had shown up in every nurse who remained kind through my pain.

He had shown up in my family's daily visits.

He had shown up in the middle of long, restless nights.

And on Day 14, He showed up in the faces of my friends.

As we talked and prayed, the song "Praise the Name of Jesus" played quietly nearby. And those words suddenly carried deeper meaning.

I realized I wasn't just surviving anymore.

I was beginning to worship again.

The sign, my family and friends, the smiles, the prayers – all of it pointed to the same truth:

God is here.

He sees me.

And He is still writing my story.

Nehemiah 8:10

*Don't be dejected and sad, for the
joy of the LORD is your strength!*

Psalm 91 (On Eagles' Wings)

"And He will raise you up on eagle's wings,
Bear you on the breath of dawn,
Make you shine like the sun,
And hold you in the palm
Of His hand."

– Shane & Shane, "Psalm 91
(On Eagles' Wings)"

*D*ay 15 was not the day I hoped for.

I felt discouraged and weary after two weeks of needing twenty-four-hour care. I was tired. Still unable to swallow. It felt as if I were walking through a long, dry valley – trying to keep my eyes lifted while feeling the weight of it all.

But as disappointment threatened to settle in, "Psalm 91" played, and it steadied me.

> "You who dwell in the shelter of the Lord,
> Who abide in His shadow for life,
> Say to the Lord, 'My refuge, my
> rock in whom I trust . . .'"

In that moment I was reminded that my healing wasn't only in the hands of surgeons – it was in the hands of the Most High. I was still under His wings. Not forgotten. Not failed. Covered.

I will rescue those who love me. I will protect those who trust in my name (Psalm 91:14).

Christine, a thoughtful and caring hospital tech, came by every day she was working. She chatted, helped, and encouraged me – and that day she washed my hair in the sink. Christine always seemed to have all the time I needed, whether bringing ice chips, adjusting pillows, or finding warm blankets. She provided comfort and care in tangible ways, and I was deeply thankful.

And then, just like they had every day before, my son and daughter arrived to spend the day with me.

In their faithfulness I saw the heart of God. I wasn't walking this path alone. My family showed up like a living Psalm 91 – a visible reminder that I was held, surrounded, and never beyond the reach of love.

Day 15 was not easy.

But even in difficulties, God was still my refuge.

Still my shelter.

Still writing my healing story – even when I couldn't see the next chapter clearly.

He's my rock – when everything else feels shaky.
He's my fortress – when the battle wears me out.
He's my deliverer – even when healing takes longer
than expected.

Psalm 18:2

*The LORD is my rock, my fortress, and my
savior; my God is my rock, in whom I find
protection. He is my shield, the power
that saves me, and my place of safety.*

Day 16

Goodness of God

"All my life You have been faithful,
All my life You have been so, so good . . ."

– Bethel Music, "Goodness of God"

By this point, the hospital had become my temporary home.

I walked the halls again – tubes, monitors, and all – still tethered but determined, while my family cheered me on. It took effort. Each step reminded me that healing was hard work, and I was doing it.

Knee therapy continued as well. It was frustrating at times, trying to strengthen a body that had been through so much. But the therapists and my family encouraged me, and I pushed through – not just for mobility but for freedom.

And through it all, I kept listening to one song on repeat:

"I love You, Lord.
Oh, Your mercy never failed me.
And all my days, I've been held in Your hands.
From the moment that I wake up
Until I lay my head,
Oh, I will sing of the goodness of God."

"Goodness of God" felt like the anthem of this journey. It wasn't just about that day; it was about every day leading up to it. Even in a hospital bed, I could look back and see His fingerprints on my life.

He had carried me through storms I once thought would break me.

He had given me a family who stayed by my side day after day.

He had placed songs in my heart when I couldn't find the words myself.

And even there, in a room full of wires and machines, His goodness was still present.

"Your goodness is running after,
it's running after me . . ."

I wasn't forgotten.
I wasn't alone.
I wasn't defeated.
His goodness followed me down the hallways.
It sat with me during therapy.
It was felt in my husband's foot massages.
It was present even in the melting of ice chips.

On Day 16, I praised Him – not for a breakthrough but for His faithfulness in the waiting.

Psalm 23:6

*Surely your goodness and unfailing love
will pursue me all the days of my life, and I
will live in the house of the LORD forever.*

Day 17

Psalm 90 (Satisfy Us with Your Love)

"When the sun comes up, satisfy us,
Before the day has passed us by,
Before our hearts forget all Your goodness,
Satisfy us with Your love."

– Shane & Shane, "Psalm 90
(Satisfy Us with Your Love)"

Today was Valentine's Day.

My son came with flowers and handmade cards and notes from the children. No candy, of course – I still couldn't have food or drink. But those flowers spoke volumes. They were a reminder of beauty, of life outside these sterile hospital walls, of love that stayed close no matter what.

We received the official results from the latest swallow test: The hole in my esophagus was still there. That news was discouraging, but it also brought clarity. The doctors decided to move forward with esophagus surgery in three days.

I tried to stay strong, but it hurt – not just physically, but emotionally and spiritually. Another surgery meant more pain, more unknowns, more nights with machines and quiet prayers in the dark. It felt like going backward, though it would hopefully bring an end to NPO (nothing by mouth).

So, we waited again.

And in the waiting, I played "Psalm 90" by Shane & Shane.

"Teach us, Lord, to number
our days on earth,
And give us more wisdom in the secret heart,
As You display amazing grace,
In Jesus Christ for us."

On Day 17, this song became my declaration of courage and peace – not the kind that denies hard news but the kind that holds tightly to hope in the middle of it.

God was still my light.

My salvation.

The stronghold of my life.

And I was not afraid.

Psalm 90:14

*Satisfy us each morning with your
unfailing love, so we may sing for
joy to the end of our lives.*

Song in the Night

"Even though I know You're able,
And I believe that You are good,
Even if You don't deliver me,
O God, You are my God."

– Shane & Shane, "Song in the Night"

Today I felt the grace of God through the people closest to me.

My daughter was by my side, bringing peace, comfort, and help in every possible way. Her presence wasn't just practical; it was deeply emotional. In a place where so much is sterile and clinical, the warmth of family reminded me that I was not alone.

She didn't try to offer empty words. She just came. She sat. She stayed. And she washed my hair in the sink. Being unable to shower was difficult, but having my hair washed lifted my spirits like nothing else.

My friend Sue also came, bringing compassion and laughter. I needed both.

My husband faithfully updated our friends each day on my progress. In return, we received texts, prayers, and Scripture from those who loved us. Some messages brought tears; others made me smile. All of them pointed me back to Jesus.

> "I will cling to the lover of my soul,
> Letting go of the rudder in the storm,
> I will call on the name of the Lord,
> You're my song in the night,
> O Jesus Christ."

"Song in the Night" by Shane & Shane resonated deeply that day. In the darkness of uncertainty and fatigue, the song reminded me that even when the night is long, God is still singing over me. During the long nights, the soft, gentle music calmed my spirit and soothed my soul.

Day 18 reminded me of a simple truth: Even here, even now, He is my song.

Psalm 42:8

But each day the LORD pours his unfailing love upon me, and through each night I sing his songs, praying to God who gives me life.

The Lord Is My Salvation

"In times of waiting, times of need
When I know loss, when I am weak . . ."

– Shane & Shane, "The Lord Is My Salvation"

Today, the journey felt especially long.

I continued walking the hospital halls, still tethered to tubes and monitors, and worked hard in knee therapy. My body was worn and weary. My fingers, arms, and abdomen were covered in bruises from weeks of injections.

The doctors came in, as they did every morning – checking my charts, reviewing scans, examining my progress, and preparing for surgery the next day. Their faces were kind but serious, always balancing encouragement with caution.

> "Who is like the Lord, our God?
> Strong to save, faithful in love.
> My debt is paid and the victory won.
> The Lord is my salvation."

I found myself clinging to every note of "The Lord Is My Salvation." The song reminded me that no matter what my body felt like or how slow the process seemed, I was not without help. The Lord is my strength. He is my deliverer. He is my hope.

Day 19 brought the same waiting. But even now, I trust.

He is my salvation.

Psalm 27:1

*The Lord is my light and my salvation,
so why should I be afraid? The Lord
is my fortress, protecting me from
danger, so why should I tremble?*

Whispering Hope

"Soft as the voice of an angel,
Breathing a lesson unheard . . ."

– Septimus Winner "Whispering Hope"

Today was the day of my esophagus surgery.

It was a hard day, full of nerves, preparation, and prayers. My husband and son were with me in pre-op, asking questions I could not ask. But one sweet moment stayed with me: My dear friend Beth had sent me the old song, "Whispering Hope." After surgery, when I returned to my room, I whispered in a soft, raspy voice to my son and daughter, "Please play 'Whispering Hope.'"

My voice was barely audible. My throat ached terribly.

I had a fresh incision in my neck, another tube inserted, and a feeding tube placed in my nose. Every breath felt like a reminder of what my body had just endured.

But that gentle melody, "Whispering Hope," was like a balm.

> "Wait till the darkness is over,
> Hope for the sunshine tomorrow . . ."

It reminded me that even in weakness, God speaks with comfort.

Even in pain, His promises are not shouted but whispered softly to our hearts.

> "Whispering hope,
> Oh, how welcome Thy voice.
> Making my heart,
> In its sorrow rejoice."

Day 20 brought weariness, pain, and no voice.

I listened.

And I believed.

Hope was still whispering to me.

Isaiah 46:4

I will be your God throughout your lifetime – until your hair is white with age. I made you, and I will care for you.

Day 21

Leaning on the Everlasting Arms

"What have I to dread, what have I to fear?
Leaning on the everlasting arms . . ."

– Selah, "Leaning on the Everlasting Arms"

After little sleep, I woke to the realization that my tubes and drains were still with me, a reminder of the discomfort when I tried to change positions. The soft music playing throughout the night was a calm refuge for my weary body and soul.

I had never taken pain medication for anything more than a migraine, but I was so thankful the nurses kept me comfortable with medication through my PICC line. Of course, they monitored carefully, always checking my chart to verify everything. Medication was a gift in this storm.

Dr. Nazarian came in and removed three of the four tubes in my back. What a wonderful surprise – I was so thankful! Now bandages covered the places where the tubes had been. I still had the feeding tube in my nose, which would remain until I successfully passed the swallow test.

Then another gift arrived: A guitarist from the hospital's music therapy program came into my room. This sweet musician asked what I would like her to play.

I asked for "Leaning on the Everlasting Arms" and "Blessed Assurance."

She sat beside my bed and began to play. The chords filled the air, and her voice rose gently above the beeping machines and clinical sounds. I could not sing along; my voice was still weak from the surgery, and the feeding tube in my nose was uncomfortable. But for a few beautiful minutes, my hospital room became a sanctuary.

> "What a fellowship, what a joy divine,
> Leaning on the everlasting arms!
> What a blessedness, what a peace is mine,
> Leaning on the everlasting arms!"

It was a time of worship.
A time of praise.
A holy interruption.

> "Leaning, leaning,
> Safe and secure from all alarms.
> Leaning, leaning,
> Leaning on the everlasting arms."

On Day 21, the gift of music encouraged me. The removal of tubes was progress. And I was leaning – truly leaning – on the everlasting arms.

Deuteronomy 33:27

The eternal God is your refuge, and his everlasting arms are under you.

Blessed Assurance

"Blessed assurance, Jesus is mine,
Oh, what a foretaste of glory divine . . ."

– Third Day, "Blessed Assurance"

The pain hadn't gone away. My throat was burning, and my voice was raspy and weak. Healing was slow. But the soft music playing in my room brought calm.

And then the hospital guitarist returned, just as she had promised.

She came to play "Blessed Assurance," the song I had requested the day before. She sat beside my bed once again and strummed the opening chords. Her voice floated gently through the air, rising above the beeping machines and the sterile hum of the hospital.

"This is my story, this is my song,
Praising my Savior all the day long . . ."

For a few sacred moments, my room was transformed into a sanctuary again.

God wasn't finished with me.

"Perfect submission, all is at rest,
I in my Savior am happy and blessed . . ."

Day 22.
This was my story.
This was my song.

Psalm 16:8

I know the LORD *is always with me. I will
not be shaken, for he is right beside me.*

Holy, Holy, Holy (We Bow before Thee)

"Holy, holy, holy,
Lord God Almighty,
Early in the morning
My song shall rise to Thee."

– Shane & Shane, "Holy, Holy,
Holy (We Bow before Thee)"

This morning began quietly – the kind of stillness that invites reflection.

I was struck by how far I had come and how far I still had to go.

Yet rather than feeling discouraged, I felt surrounded by holiness. Not because of where I was but because of who God is.

My son and daughter continued working as they sat in my room, stepping out when necessary to make phone calls or grab something to eat. They listened carefully when doctors and nurses came in and asked questions I didn't know to ask. They offered to stay through the night, but still being Mom, I knew they needed good, uninterrupted sleep so they could remain alert during the day. I thanked God daily for them – for their presence, their love, and the precious gift they are to me.

As I listened during the night, the hymn "Holy, Holy, Holy" filled my room – a powerful reminder that even in the most clinical, uncomfortable, and vulnerable moments, God is still enthroned in glory. Still sovereign. Still worthy. And He was with me even when my family was not.

> "Lord, only Thou art holy,
> There is none beside Thee,
> Perfect in power,
> Love and purity."

I whispered the lyrics along with the music, my voice faint but full of reverence.

On Day 23, I knew He had not changed.

He had not left.

Psalm 3:3

But you, O LORD, are a shield around me; you are my glory, the one who holds my head high.

Living Hope

"Then came the morning that
sealed the promise,
Your buried body began to breathe . . ."

– Phil Wickham, Living Hope

*T*oday, I held on to hope with everything I had.

I was still weak, still unable to eat or drink. My vocal cords were damaged, and the healing journey felt slow and unpredictable. But even in that, I could feel life returning in small, quiet ways – a little more strength in my steps, a little less fear in my heart.

Erica and Virginia were with me today. The encouragement and distraction they brought helped the long days pass faster.

As I listened to "Living Hope" by Phil Wickham, I was reminded that my hope was not in doctors or treatments or even in the passing of time.

"Hallelujah, praise the One who set me free,
Hallelujah, death has lost its grip on me,
You have broken every chain,
There's salvation in Your name,
Jesus Christ, my living hope."

My hope is in a risen Savior.

He has conquered the grave.

He has overcome the darkness.

And He is with me here – in this room, in this body, in this moment.

On Day 24, I held on to hope – and I knew I was not alone.

Jesus Christ, my living hope.

Psalm 63:8

*I cling to you; your strong right
hand holds me securely.*

Day 25

Love of God

"It's so good I almost can't believe it,
Far beyond what hearts could ever dream,
The God who set the galaxies in motion
Would descend to give His life for me."

– Brandon Lake & Phil
Wickham, "Love of God"

Today I felt wrapped in the steady warmth of God's love.

It's hard to explain how deeply the love of God comforted me during this long journey – not just as a concept or memory but as something present, holding me, healing me, and sustaining me.

I received a sweet and unexpected gift. My dear friend Jen, from out of state, came to visit, encourage, and pray with me. Seeing her face brought comfort and smiles. I didn't have the energy for many visitors, but this dear prayer partner brought me hope and love.

I played "Love of God" by Brandon Lake and Phil Wickham, and the lyrics poured into my soul like medicine.

> "Singing, 'Oh, how great is the love of God,
> He paid our debt on that rugged cross,
> For all our days, we will sing our Savior's praise,
> How great is the love of God . . .'"

Even with the pain.
Even with the feeding tubes.
Even with the slow progress.
I was not forgotten.
I was not alone.
I was deeply loved.

> "This all my life, the banner I'll be waving,
> My anthem cry, no matter what may come,
> And when I rise to walk the streets of heaven,
> I'll still be singing this song (oh, my song),
> For everything that You've done,
> How great the love of God . . ."

That truth carried me through Day 25. I may have been physically weak, but I was emotionally strengthened because God's love never fails, never runs out, and never lets go.

Jeremiah 31:25

*For I have given rest to the weary
and joy to the sorrowing.*

I Speak Jesus

"I just want to speak the name of Jesus,
Over every heart and every mind,
'Cause I know there is peace
within Your presence,
I speak Jesus."

– Charity Gayle, "I Speak Jesus"

Tomorrow held another swallow test.

I had been down this road before, and the outcome weighed heavily on my heart. I wanted to be hopeful, but I couldn't ignore the anxiety pressing in. Had my esophagus finally healed after the surgery? My body was tired – but my spirit still longed for good news.

This test would determine if I could begin eating. After twenty-five days without enjoying food or liquids by mouth, I was very eager for good news.

Today, I played "I Speak Jesus" by Charity Gayle, and

it helped reframe my thoughts. I paused and remembered what Jesus had already done – not just for my
body but for my soul.

> "Your name is power.
> Your name is healing.
> Your name is life.
> Break every stronghold.
> Shine through the shadows.
> Burn like a fire."

His blood has already purchased my healing.

His sacrifice has already made a way.

No matter what tomorrow's test shows, the greatest
healing has already happened.

On Day 26, I was covered by grace. I was seen. I
was loved.

And I was thankful.

2 Corinthians 12:9

*Each time he said, "My grace is all you need.
My power works best in weakness." So now I
am glad to boast about my weaknesses, so that
the power of Christ can work through me.*

Day 27

In Christ Alone

"In Christ alone my hope is found,
He is my light, my strength, my song . . ."

– Shane & Shane, "In Christ Alone"

Today was a day to reflect—on how far I had come, how much I had endured, and how deeply I had needed Jesus every step of the way.

It had been nearly a month since my hospitalization began, and though my body was still recovering, my heart was anchored. The trials had tested me in ways I never imagined, but through it all I had found one unshakable truth: Christ is enough.

When fear tried to overwhelm me, when pain made me cry out, when hope felt far away, He was near. He had always been there. He would not let go.

My son and daughter were also near and faithfully stayed with me. They continued to work from my room as time allowed, but if I needed them, they were ready to be at my side. I was so thankful for the love and dedication of my family. They were a comfort and a help, always ready to listen carefully to doctors' explanations and instructions.

As I was wheeled in for the swallow test, I felt both apprehensive and hopeful. The technician was thorough, though a bit quicker than during previous tests, and I was asked to swallow sips of different solutions. I knew it would be a day or two before the official results came back, so I tried to stay positive yet realistic.

> "From life's first cry to final breath,
> Jesus commands my destiny . . ."

On Day 27, I hummed softly along with the music playing at my bedside, unable to sing the words out loud but believing every one.

> "In Christ alone my hope is found."

And He had never let me down.

Isaiah 41:13

> *For I hold you by your right hand – I,*
> *the LORD your God. And I say to you,*
> *"Don't be afraid. I am here to help you."*

Day 28

His Mercy Is More

"Praise the Lord.
His mercy is more.
Stronger than darkness,
New every morn.
Our sins they are many,
His mercy is more."

– Shane & Shane, "His Mercy Is More"

oday brought amazing news – the kind of break-through we had all been praying for.

The results from my swallow test came back:

The hole in my esophagus was closed!

Tears filled my eyes. After weeks of being unable to eat or drink, the doctors said I could begin having thick liquids. A simple step to many, but for me it was monumental. My nose feeding tube was removed. I was a little nervous but also ready for the next step.

Then for the first time in 28 days, I breathed fresh air. My tubes and wires were temporarily disconnected and Michael helped me into a wheelchair. He covered me in blankets, and took me to a beautiful courtyard where we spent a few minutes enjoying the outdoors and sunshine. A delightful respite.

The dietician and speech therapist came to my room and explained what my new "meals" would look like. They described the textures, the precautions, and the process of slowly reintroducing food. I listened carefully, almost in disbelief that I had finally reached this point.

Then, at dinnertime, a tray arrived: soup, thickened orange juice, and yogurt.

It might as well have been a feast.

I closed my eyes and savored every bite, whispering thanks to Jesus with every spoonful. I had to swallow with a "chin tuck" – my chin on my chest to aid correct swallowing. With every tuck I whispered, "Thank you, Lord. Heal me."

But today also held deep sorrow. We received news that my precious mother-in-law had passed away.

Her absence felt heavy. She was a one-of-a-kind, determined, and confident woman. She will be greatly missed.

My husband left to be with family, and though I would miss him in the coming days, I knew this was where he needed to be.

As I sat in my room, surrounded by both comfort and grief, I played "His Mercy Is More." The lyrics carried me back through every hard moment of this journey.

Through every night and every breakthrough.

Through every tube and every tear.

They resonated deeply with this moment of gratitude and surrender.

This journey had been long and painful, but following Jesus – even here – had led me to healing.

On Day 28, I knew this truth: He is worth it all.

Psalm 100:5

For the LORD is good. His unfailing love continues forever, and his faithfulness continues to each generation.

It's Always Been You

"You are the voice that calms
the storm inside me,
Castle walls that stand around me,
All this time, my guardian was You.
You are the light that shines in every tunnel,
There in the past, You'll be there tomorrow,
All my life, Your love was breaking through."

– Phil Wickham, "It's Always Been You"

Today I was moved to a new room, out of PCU and onto a different floor of the hospital. The room was large, and bright sunlight poured in through the window like a quiet gift. Once again, the nurses were so kind, answering every question, explaining every change, and treating me with such dignity and care.

Because of my healing esophagus, some of my medications could now be taken by mouth. But there was a catch: The pills had to be crushed and mixed with applesauce. I never imagined I would be so grateful for applesauce.

Every meal – still made up of thick liquids – tasted wonderful. I learned that joy is found in the smallest things: warm soup, a smooth spoonful of yogurt, the first sip of something that didn't come through a tube.

"It's always been You."

And it always will be.

On Day 29, after twenty-eight days, I was eating by mouth – settled in a new room and filled with peace.

John 14:27

I am leaving you with a gift – peace
of mind and heart. And the peace I
give is a gift the world cannot give.
So don't be troubled or afraid.

How Great Thou Art

"Then sings my soul, my Savior God, to Thee,
How great Thou art, how great Thou art . . ."

– Shane & Shane, "How Great Thou Art"

Today, as I walked in the hall outside my room, I noticed a large wall – a quiet, powerful reminder of faith. The wall was covered with a variety of crosses: wooden, metal, simple, ornate – each one a symbol of hope, sacrifice, and strength.

Each cross told a story, just like mine: a story of struggle, surrender, and healing.

In the midst of these hospital walls, surrounded by tubes, monitors, and daily challenges, the crosses spoke to me. They reminded me of the depth of God's love and the greatness of His power to save and restore.

I played "How Great Thou Art"[1] by Shane & Shane and let the soaring melody lift my spirit.

Even in this place, even on this hard journey, my soul could still sing.

On Day 30, I reflected on stories of hope.

How great is our God.

Psalm 89:1

I will sing of the LORD's unfailing love forever!
Young and old will hear of your faithfulness.

Bless God

"Bless God, for He holds the victory.
Bless God, for He's always with me.
Bless God, for He's always worthy.
Every chance I get, I'll bless Your name."

– Brooke Ligertwood, "Bless God"

Today was a day of mixed emotions.

After thirty-one days of hospital stays, surgeries, and healing, the doctors finally cleared me to go home. Dr. Kristi arrived in my room and discussed the plans for my physical therapy and speech therapy. As I sat in the recliner, this precious friend prayed with me again. My PICC line was removed, and I felt free. I was filled with gratitude and relief to leave the hospital walls behind and return to familiar surroundings. I would have months of therapy for my body and speech therapy for my damaged vocal cord, but I would be praising God for every step of progress.

But my heart was heavy.

This was also the day of my mother-in-law's funeral, a woman who was a cherished part of our family. I was deeply saddened that I could not be there in person to say goodbye and honor her memory.

Still, even in the midst of grief, I chose to bless God –

For His faithfulness through every challenge.

For the strength to face each day.

For the hope that sustains me beyond the pain.

I played "Bless God" by Brooke Ligertwood as I prepared to leave, singing praise over what God had done in my life and holding tightly to His promises for the future.

Day 31 was not the end of my story but the beginning of a new chapter – one marked by healing, hope, and the unwavering presence of God.

Psalm 89:52

Praise the LORD forever! Amen and amen!

My thirty-one days in the hospital were filled with pain, uncertainty, and moments I never expected to face. Yet through it all, I discovered something profound: God's presence is real, steady, and life-giving – even in the darkest valleys.

Christian music became more than comfort; it became a lifeline. Each song wove courage, hope, and peace into my weary heart when my body and spirit felt weak. The lyrics spoke truths I needed to hear, even when I couldn't pray the words myself. The melodies lifted my soul and reminded me who was holding me long before I could hold on to anything else.

This journey taught me several lasting truths:

- Waiting is not wasted time but an act of faith.

- Healing comes in seasons, not on a schedule.

- Community – family, friends, and caregivers – is a tangible expression of God's love.

- Even in suffering, worship is a powerful act of surrender and strength.

As I move forward, I carry these lessons in my heart. I know there will be challenges ahead, but I also know the One who walks beside me.

If you are facing your own battle – whether in a hospital bed, in your mind, or in your soul – I hope my story and these songs remind you:

You are not alone.

God is fighting for you.

His love will never let go.

May you find your own anthem, your own hope, and your own peace.

Because in the end, whatever the battle may be, the victory belongs to the Lord.

Thank You

My deepest and sincere thanks to:

My Lord and Savior Jesus Christ, who has a plan for my life, has numbered my days, and loves me more than I can understand.

My dear husband, Sam, for his constant love, devotion, and foot rubs.

My children – Erica, Michael, and Andrew – and my in-loves Steve, Virginia, and Shelby, for your prayers, support, and the endless hours you spent with me: listening to the doctors, getting me ice chips, sleeping in cold recliners, and helping me in every situation.

My grandchildren – Elizabeth, Anna, Nate, Hope, Luke, Hadleigh, Hudson, Hunter, Liam, and Maisie – for praying for their Nana.

Dr. Nazarian, Dr. Pond, Baylor All Saints Hospital, Kristi Harring, PA, Christine Balthrop, and the incredible nurses and aides who cared for me.

Precious friends who fed my family while I was in the hospital and lovingly brought meals when I came home.

My dear friends all over the world who prayed for me!

Jeremiah Zeiset and Aneko Press for encouraging me and believing in my attempt to document this journey.

My 31-Day Hospital Playlist

1. "Battle Belongs" – Phil Wickham

2. "'Tis So Sweet" – Shane & Shane

3. "He Will Hold Me Fast" – Shane & Shane

4. "I Will Wait for You (Psalm 130)" – Shane & Shane

5. "Psalm 46 (Lord of Hosts)" – Shane & Shane

6. "Hope Has a Name" – River Valley Worship

7. "In Christ Alone" – Shane & Shane

8. "Psalm 23 (Surely Goodness, Surely Mercy)"
   – Shane & Shane

9. "Give Me Jesus" – Shane & Shane

10. "Psalm 139 (Far Too Wonderful)" – Shane & Shane

11. "No One Ever Cared for Me Like Jesus"
    – Steffany Gretzinger

12. "Only There" – Shane & Shane

13. "Where I'm Standing Now" – Phil Wickham

14. "Praise the Name of Jesus" – Shane & Shane

15. "Psalm 91 (On Eagles' Wings)" – Shane & Shane

16. "Goodness of God" – Bethel Music

17. "Psalm 90 (Satisfy Us with Your Love)" – Shane & Shane

18. "Song in the Night" – Shane & Shane

19. "The Lord Is My Salvation" – Shane & Shane

20. "Whispering Hope" – Anne Murray

21. "Leaning on the Everlasting Arms" – Selah

22. "Blessed Assurance" – Third Day

23. "Holy, Holy, Holy (We Bow before Thee)" – Shane & Shane

24. "Living Hope" – Phil Wickham

25. "Love of God" – Brandon Lake & Phil Wickham

26. "I Speak Jesus" – Charity Gayle

27. "In Christ Alone" – Shane & Shane

28. "His Mercy Is More" – Shane & Shane

29. "It's Always Been You" – Phil Wickham

30. "How Great Thou Art" – Shane & Shane

31. "Bless God" – Brooke Ligertwood

- "A Thousand Hallelujahs" – Brooke Ligertwood

- "What He's Done" – Passion

- "One Day (When We All Get to Heaven)" – The Worship Initiative

- "I Am Not Alone" – Kari Jobe

Full Playlist on Spotify

https://open.spotify.com/playlist/38MatsZw2gFSRIXxPV joFx?si

About the Author

Susan Ferguson and her husband, Sam, live in Mansfield, Texas and enjoy living close to their three married children and ten grandchildren. Susan, a retired teacher, loves reading, sourdough baking, and of course, listening to music. She has also lived in England, California, Italy, and Florida and believes *For I can do everything through Christ who gives me strength* (Philippians 4:13).